RITA SUMMERS

SELECTED POEMS

Print ISBN: 978-1-66787-778-5

Cover photography by Rita Summers and Charlotte Noyes

Table of Contents

Words, Words, Words, Words, Words

Words
channels of words
that constrain the flow of thought
through the wild river of consciousness

Words
chains of words
that bind the mind's chaos
that break its silence

Words
cords of words
that wrap around memory
that change it or strangle it

Words
that sometimes cooperate
with a dumb whim
to make a poem

Being Helen Keller at Whaler's Cove

I feel hot sun on my arms
I feel the tingle of cool breeze on warm skin
I smell sagebrush
I smell cypress

I feel the shade of a pine and
the smell of its resin
As I walk along this cove,
I feel the force it takes to walk uphill,
I feel the mass of a passing car

I try to be Helen Keller
With poison oak on my left,
cars on my right,
I can't close my eyes
With only a light cap,
I can't block my ears,
but I try to be Helen Keller

Subtract sight and hearing
Subtract the stunning blue of the water,
Subtract its shadows, ripples, islands of kelp
Subtract the sightings of gulls, grebes, herons
Subtract the cries, the splash of wing on water
Subtract the wind in the pines
Subtract the rhythmic whoosh of waves

Add power to what survives
Add a surpassing sensibility that can
sense green from soft earth of a field
sense music from fingers in a brook

Add a newer potent sense –
words -
flowing through hands, through fingertips
opening, connecting –
to whalers and divers,
to clouds, cliffs, gulls in flight,
gardens under water,

to the fullness of being
at Whalers Cove

Mustard Flowers

They lean across my path this August day,
yellow blossoms at tips of long thin stems

Their sharp tang cuts to my dormant core -
to childhood fields, to tangled scents of
licorice, mint, and mustard flower –

alien weed, and native weed too

Wildflowers as Fibonacci Series

Thrift and
Sea pinks
and Seathrift
California thrift
Armeria maritima
All of these are names for the same small pale pink flower

Planning for Serendipity

Scientists, I hear, now try to
plan for serendipity

Plan for the unplanned
Why not?
Chance is too chancy
to leave to chance

But chance is just the hand
that opens the cellar door,
releasing discovery, insight -
those bright bubbles of a
brew that's made from
    grainy observation,
    in yeasty incubation,
    stirred by reflection,
    fermented long and slow
in the hidden lower levels
of the mind

Death Valley, Early February

Warm room, books, deck of cards,
the two of us together in
long desert winter nights
I need nothing more,
I want nothing more

Winter-break trip - one of many -
in a work schedule followed for fifteen years

The desert now is cold, pure, simple,
visitors few, amusements few
We walk to breakfast exhaling vapor,
our shadows sharp,
past horses, an empty pool, rows of smoke trees
Our hotel, called the Ranch, seems just that
We eat with cowboys and Indians,
who work here

Days we're on the trail
boots on sand and stone
eyes on jagged rocks, sculpted rocks
cream and pink and gold and mauve
Roadrunners streak by,
quail families parade

Or on the road, seeing the sights -
old borax mines,
rare pupfish in pool,
the improbable Scotty's Castle,
the impossible beauty of the dunes
decorated by wind-made ripples and
snake-made tracings

I want to stay here and
never go back
to work,
complexity,
real life

We take the back way out through
softly curving Panamint Mountains,
find a motel in Lone Pine,
drive to Whitney Portal,
step onto the empty Mt. Whitney trail,
shivering in semi-dark under towering peaks

Then drinks, steak dinner, back
to our little room

A good trip - one of many,
one of many

The Last Time

The last time will come,
some time, for each
cherished nub of us; or,
the last time *has* come

You in front of me,
with hat and canteen,
pounding down the trail
in the light and air of late
afternoon

Evenings at the jogging track,
sea breeze and pines

Pancakes on Sunday morning,
a joyful joining

Long walks through foreign cities,
our hand-in-hand adventure

Your astute crack about the news,
your tears about the news

The poem you read to me
The song you sing to me

9

The Bequest

The man I loved has gone,
bequeathing to my care
another man who looks just like him

I love him too, or so it seems
Why else my daily visits
just to sit by him or feed him snacks
or wheel him around –
first to the patio to visit our pine -
a seedling when we came here,
now twice my height -
then, through the secured door
to living room, library, lobby,
bistro for coffee and, with luck,
someone I can talk to
and he can listen to

I can talk to the new man but
he does not talk to me
He knows me in some way but
I seem to hold no special place in
his mind or memory or heart

A foreign-born friend,
mixing up military medals,
says that I deserve a purple heart
That is true

I am wounded, and my heart
pumps a purple mix –
blue for blues,
red for stubborn love

Watching a Documentary Film: Crying with One Eye

Over 100 years old,
tough and tiny
At her grand piano, she plays each one each day -
each precious piece that she knows by heart

Over 90,
slim and agile
She seems to float over her abstract canvas
as she adds thick red and gold

Over 80,
compact and poised
before her flower arrangement, she considers
a change, makes it, then unmakes it

Over 70,
wondering and pondering,
I weep as I watch
these women on the screen

Tears of joy and hope
for what can be
Tears of rage and anguish
for what cannot

I cry with my left eye only
I try to keep the right eye
dry and clear to see ahead

I Want to Dance

We're out of step
I want to dance and you
are sitting out this dance,
maybe all the rest

You say you want to dance
I don't know if you do,
I don't know if you can
dance with me, or even
dance alone, to your own tune

You once wrote tunes - you have a gift
You like to watch dancing on TV –
your window to the world out there

You like to catch what comes -
Bonds are down, a standoff in Iraq,
new finding - wine prolongs life,
the Marx brothers, Mrs. Miniver

Stifled, bored, cold, achy,
stranded in a stupid little town,
air no good to breathe
That's what you say
No wonder you won't dance

I want to help you walk,
don't know if I can, but

I want to dance

Walking Behind You

A little behind you
on the flat seashore trail
I match my pace to your
slow unsteady steps
Soft air bathes my face and
coastal scrub emits a minty tang

Out together,
out of the closed house;
this is rare now

My thoughts tread another trail -
one of those we knew by heart
On our left, river leaping over rocks
On our right, pine forest where
late day wind plays and sings

Down the canyon, familiar last leg,
the steep ascents behind us,
all downhill now,
I follow you in
rapid pounding descent,
mind vacant but for
water, pine, stone and wind,
your faded blue jacket,
your old red day pack

Body and mind ache to be there
I must be, I need to be, I want to be
here - half a step behind
               ≈

Kindness

Kind –
of a sympathetic nature
disposed to be helpful and solicitous –
the dictionary says

Just the other day
my husband was told
by someone kind that
I was kind

Not a word I would apply to me
Never considered a career in
doctoring or nursing
Never took in a stray cat
or tried to mend a broken wing

I am just your standard selfish person,
but perhaps an observer cannot see that,
cannot distinguish me from a kind person

I am just a standard person with
kindness thrust upon her

≈

Summer Haiku

Six piles of fresh earth
One cat - poised, curved paw lifted
Where are you, gopher?

≈

Boards over white sand
In a crack, safely sheltered,
one yellow poppy

≈

Across the cove's rocks,
white in the midday sun, flies
a flock of shadows

≈

Haiku. For Illia

Born small, in cold, you
grew - warm in new name and place,
now still grow, give, warm

≈

15

Looking in the Garage

Maybe if we reinvent whatever our lives give us
we find poems. Check your garage, the odd sock
in your drawer, the person you almost like, but not quite.
And let me know. Naomi Shihab Nye

Naomi, it's true
the poems have been hiding

So I'll try the garage -
where life's traces reside
filed in steel or
shelved in coded cardboard

When I break the tape
will they leap out and reproach me
for decades of neglect?
Or will they embrace me and
pour into me so that
I can pour them on the page?
Or will they just sit mute,
passive papers that they are?

This carton holds ancient tax returns,
good for a sonnet perhaps
on the romance of student poverty

Two steel cabinets, bright blue,
bought for our house that lacked closets
I once wrote an ode to that neighborhood

In one cabinet, figurines my mother loved –
Dutch boy and girl flirting through their glazes –
Tablecloth for special occasions
What wine stains its soft green damask?
What words did the boy and girl overhear?

A two-wheeled cart -
I used it at the farmers' market
when hands and arms hurt too much
to carry anything
Combine it with the detailed time log
in carton K14 for a lament on authorship
This drawer holds maps -
London underground, Madrid, Rome
Trails of Mammoth Lakes,
Treasures of Los Angeles -
for visitors to the 1984 Olympics
Joshua Tree park – yes! Desert!

Some winter day
I'll write a desert poem
full of sun and sky and spring bloom,
full of love and longing,
and I'll let you know, Naomi

≈

Savings Bonds

On the way to my favorite walk
I stopped at the post office
and found a check I was expecting -
return address: Federal Reserve,
real sender: my parents,
real postmark: soon after World War Two

I put the check in my pocket and
came here to the edge of the land

The beach is full and festive -
it's Labor Day weekend
Kids dump sand into bright buckets
or wade out ankle-deep
Black turnstones poke in thick stacks of kelp -
sour, half-rotten, full of edible treasure

A rustle reminds me of the check -
proceeds from redeemed bonds,
the grandchildren of bonds
my parents bought sixty years ago,
when they were vigorous, both working,
and had saved some money,
and had no idea that they were
sending a gift into the next century,
into this year of their 100th birthdays
into this place,

where the sea breeze
now dries my tears

≈

Found Haiku: On Morning Traffic Report

CHP reports
someone sitting and praying
in the far right lane

≈

Haiku. This Coastline I Often Walk

My hat, shoes, jacket
always the same, while each day
it wears brand new waves

≈

Harvest Moon

I moved north and
the moon moved too

Before, it rose over junipers
(or, on clear cold nights, over remote white peaks)
Its ascent crossed the descent of jet planes

After, it rose over low hills and
instantly cast its image onto the bay
to pave a golden road or
shatter into scintillating shapes

Once (it was soon after moving)
I walked toward the bay and
another walker said *harvest moon*

It was just that moment fully risen -
a warm giant, glowing red-gold, and
unrolling a bright carpet straight to me

The same familiar moon -
in this new place magnified,
in this new time ripe with meaning,

lighting my way into
harvest time

≈

Two Gardens

Russell Square contains a pleasant symmetry and a few refined features that encourage diverse yet serene activity. Website of the Project for Public Spaces.

Point Lobos is a natural reserve, not a park, and afforded the highest level of statewide protection. The ...purpose of a reserve is to forever protect an area of unique natural beauty and ecological significance. Website of the Pt. Lobos Foundation

Mid-April 1966

First giddy hours in London,
the British Museum at opening time,
hotel room overlooking Russell Square –
cold and colorless under gray sky,
branches bare and black,
a few white crocus
soon there will be daffodils then tulips,
buds on trees, then deep green chestnut leaves

Mid-April 2007

Point Lobos, Central California coast
Crowded this bright Monday -
locals, touring Minnesota birders,
families from Europe,
children not dreamed of,
parents not yet born
that London spring

In a still clear aqua cove,
sheltered by swirls of kelp,
a slippery gray seal pup tries and tries
to stay on its mother's back

On offshore rocks cormorants
turn every surface into black motion
Flying in with beaks full of
kelp for lining nests
flying off for kelp and fish
A few sit serenely on nests
Pairs circle each other,
lift both wings, look big;
iridescent throats match the sea below,
silky white plumes lift in the wind

Amid blackness a few white highlights -
gulls on their nests
On the ledge below, a Canada Goose
rises, pokes gently at two giant eggs
A lone heron, nearly invisible in stillness and
soft color, is suddenly, vividly aloft

The flat seaside promontory swarms with
poppies of every possible yellow, gold, orange
nodding to each other, to visitors and cameras

Poking out from sagebrush and coyote brush
tiny flowers - a multitude of types
 – just a few of each –
pale blue, yellow, lavender, pink, white
most native, many from Europe

The garden of my London spring –
where white crocuses bloomed -
was laid out two centuries ago
It was lately redone with
curved pathways, benches, lawns
a cafe, fountains, new shrubs and flowers

My two gardens survive and thrive -
one by plan, construction, and care,
one by protected freedom to be itself

≈

Quiet

Quiet is an elusive treasure

I live alone in a quiet place, but
hours of news and books and music
stream through my headphones,
and, when I pull those off,
my own mind streams endless chatter

When I walk by the sea,
I am just there – just aware -
aware of sun and breeze on my face
aware of the trail's ups and downs,
aware of fog taking turns with sunshine,
aware of the sound of the surf

And that steady wordless awareness -
maybe that is my quiet

≈

My Letter to the World

To the people of the world I say:
mend your ways and do it soon

Desist from war and empire
Leave outer space out there
Devote yourselves to this earth -
already far beyond our understanding

Know one another
Cherish one another
Provide for one another

Join to know and nurture
this rich tender earth,
this violent vulnerable earth

≈

Ode to Lace Lichen

Your delicate look deceives -
loose lace pattern, pale green strands
draped and softly swaying on
branches – dead branches
where more light falls

You are simple, not even a plant,
a wrapping of fungus and algae

You live on light and water
nothing else
You ride on wind,
hitchhike with birds

What you gather from passing air –
dust, nitrogen, salt, carbon, sulfur –
you release to falling rain
and it feeds your tree
You clean the air, but
if it is too dirty, you die

If wind or rain tears you down,
you feed animals
If you lack water
you play dead decades until,
watered, you revive
You live, lace lichen, as a
benign cleansing breath
Teach us how

Ode to the Ground Beneath Us

Ground, you give me
steady support underfoot
and here, beside the bay,
in dazzling sun after rain,
your trail sparkles with
random bits of abalone shell

Ground, you wear many skins -

right here dirt and gravel over granite
right now strong and stable

elsewhere
white sand dune
kelp-draped gravel
dark velvet moss
mangrove swamp
deep redwood duff
gleaming glacial polish
cupped alpine lake
meadow of tiny blooms
ocean waves

Ground, you slide and slip and
pour molten red into the sea,
shaking and breaking old skin,
greedy to grow new skin

Ground, we clothe you
and we scar you -
rows of corn
road of hewn stone
cobblestone street
black asphalt road
concrete freeway, and
oil field

But these are aberrations
You quite dependably house us
while we live and also after

Here you glisten with
millennia of shellfish meals
Near here, you cover
bones of ancient ancestors that
rest on much more ancient
bones of your ancestors

By happy chance, dear ground
you came to be - and
we to walk on you
By clear choice, dear people
let us tread softly

≈

Equanimity at Point Lobos

Temperature mild, breeze gentle, sky cloudless,
fall equinox approaching

Far offshore sits a fog bank,
dark gray, solid as a steel bar
From Whalers Knoll rises gray smoke -
no! – a fragment of fog

At equinox, day and night are equal
It is a time of balance
On that day, it was said,
an egg could stand upright

The hard fog bank offshore softens
Its top roughens, and chunks break off,
then float toward land
Cliffs to the south disappear

Later, long ribbons of gray fog
stretch to Monastery Beach
Soon fog and sun will be
in perfect balance and so
for a moment – egglike – am I

≈

I Thought My Life Was Over

I thought my life was over
An evil disease had descended
on the man I loved and lived life with
No longer could I deny
or even doubt

But I was wrong
My life was not over

Slowly, carefully, I untangled strands
from the knotted skein of our life

Slowly, learning, I spun new strands
from new wool

Slowly, I wove a fabric
I like its looks
I hope it wears well

≈

Baby Seals at China Cove

All born these last few weeks
There's safety in numbers - but
it's not absolute

As I watch from above,
pups find teats and mothers move
between beach and sea,
pups riding on their backs
or following behind

One pair swims in translucid turquoise water,
others rest on the bright solid sand

A turkey vulture arcs by
at my eye level,
head blood red

At the back of the deep cove
four vultures tear at the remains
of a pup's flesh

I move to a new viewpoint
The deep end now hidden,
I watch the peaceful nursery

≈

Delayed Implantation

More rape than love, it seems
for a female sea otter
Forced underwater, gasping for breath
nose battered and bloody from grasping claws
But later they hang out for days,
a floating and eating pair,
until he leaves

An embryo may result -
victory for this fragile species
too much for the individual
worn out from raising her last pup –
a year or more of gestation and care –
feeding, holding, grooming, teaching
diving for food for two

So the embryo floats in limbo
until the time is right for its mother,
until she is well-fed, rested, sleek in fur
Then it settles in and starts to grow

As for otters, so for human invention -
new drug, song, software, poem
From the fierce intercourse of life and work
comes an embryo that floats submerged
until suddenly, as if by chance, it surfaces and
settles into the conscious mind

≈

Three Degrees of Separation

In a palatial new home within a hillside enclave
that overlooks a scenic river valley
lives (part-time) a captain of industry,
who showed his new home to a neighbor,
who works as a personal trainer and
who twice a week chats and consults with a caregiver,
who then drives to his home near strawberry fields and
who recently helped out a young strawberry picker
who, waiting for the season to start, slept under a bridge

≈

Clarity, Clean and Perfect

Clarity, under a dark blue sky

Each wave, each cloud, each sparkling rock,
each bird cry, each tiny golden petal,
the air I breathe -
all are clear, clean, perfect

The only human traces are the trail, weathered fences,
two small fishing boats, and a tall white sail

If only I could bottle this clarity and
scrub the muddy windshield through which
we see and steer our human world

≈

Clarity

The year ends today in brilliance -
dark blue sea stretching to a far
sharp horizon of rare clarity,
tide lowest I have ever seen here -
waders ankle deep way out,
flat beach revealing its hidden extent

My personal horizon is clearer too -
it's one year nearer, of course -
and, wondrously, I secured this year
a beachhead near here

I will walk along this shore
as long as my legs allow
and each walk will be in a new place
that has never been before

≈

Mast Years

*Every 5 or so years, oak trees produce an extra-large crop of
acorns. Although this is a huge effort, the abundance of
acorns means that predators cannot eat all of them, so
many more
germinate and begin to grow. And predators reproduce so
much that they starve the following year.*

This earth is hot - from trapped sun-heat,
from the heat of human bodies -
eight billion busy growing, mining, making,
shipping, buying, using, trashing

On a park bench perched on
the backbone of a little peninsula
I feel no heat, only cool morning air

The ground is drought-dusty but
oaks and pines carry on; acorns and cones abound,
woodpeckers, jays, and squirrels respond
The pines, long without rain, are bravely green
In fog, a nourishing rain falls from
their soaked hangings of lace lichen

Some sunny weeks later the ground is
padded with oak leaves and pine needles,
dotted with fallen needle bundles
Oak leaves are dull and every pine is part brown,
one that I know well alarmingly brown
Trees and ground are thick with acorns,
with scurrying, climbing, jumping squirrels,
The air resounds with woodpecker pounding

The oaks keep ancient tricks up their bark -
like extreme swings in acorn crop,
so acorn-eaters multiply wildly one year
and starve the next

Like jays and squirrels, we are predators -
keen and many - feasting on air, water, oil, and acorns,
counting on mast years

To mend our ways,
and we must,
we will need
the cunning of oak
and the wisdom of lichen

≈

Que Sera Sera

Star student at Adult Day Care,
Robert is grizzled, with drooping nose,
crooked teeth, and radiant smile

They sit at a round table -
six seniors and one young aide
Love Me or Leave Me... sings Doris Day

Que sera sera she sings
and Robert sings with her

> I heard her sing it once
> Ah, memories
> I was in the Army
> Que sera sera

How long were you in the Army?

> Twenty-seven years. Ah memories.
> Que sera sera

> I was in Germany then
> You should have heard it
> Two hundred soldiers singing
> Que sera sera
> Two hundred soldiers singing
> Que sera sera

≈

My Grandmother's Hands

No ring or polish marred
her honest fingers -
wrinkled, swollen, scarred
by a life no harder than many,
but hard

Her hands stirred my porridge,
soothed my cuts and burns

Her hands hauled grocery bags,
wielded the heavy old knife to
cut the hunk of meat, the whole chicken

Her hands crocheted, knitted, held cards,
held a tall glass of tea with lemon,
held a cigarette – just one – after dinner,
danced in air as she talked with friends

Her hands covered her eyes when she despaired,
then stroked the dog who came to comfort her,
and when she sat and rested, her
moistened finger turned page after page

≈

This Fog

I often walk here on the dunes on
the west coast of our continent

Life abounds here -
in the sea, on the shore, in the air –
in rare beauty, in rare diversity

Often, I see whales,
following their ancient routes

Often the light reflected off
white sand is fiercely bright
Often, out at sea, below clear blue sky,
a gray bank of fog waits its turn
Often the fog envelops all and
cypresses become blurred shadows
Often, I see the fog break up at noon,
a victory of light, of clarity

Today's fog is unfamiliar, puzzling -
an amorphous brown-gray beast
crouched just offshore, as if
pinned by the extra weight of
smoke from recent fires

This fog will soon shake itself and
move in

This fog will chill my bones
but I will keep walking
          ≈

Asilomar, Then and Now

The conference session ends at four and a
chattering wave of people rolls beachward
We hear, then see, the sea
The human wave is suddenly silent

We have a wide-open view
to either side, framed by points
to south and far north,
a distinct horizon far ahead
It is cloudy but crystal-clear

The winter sun is low,
descending behind layers of cloud
that thin at lower levels until
the lowest level is cloudless and
a strip of gray sky touches water

The sinking sun turns the sky from
varied gray to a warm glow of color,
then it's in our eyes, then it's gone
and then the glow is gone

I am overcome, not just by
sea and sky, by all of it:
stark architecture of black rocks,
low coastal scrub, sand dunes,
wind-flattened cypresses,
wind-twisted pines that grow sideways,
giant pines that grow up and out,
gulls and cormorants, seals and otters,
blended smell of pine and sea

My love and I return,
again and again,
over fifteen years,
then we come to stay
and start a new life

Twenty years later, as an
old and new widow, I walk daily
in the depth of winter,
easing grief and disarray

One day I come here at four -
clear gray sky, low sun
behind layers of cloud
Suddenly, surprised, I am
seeing with my former eyes and
feeling with my former heart
My stricken core is consoled
and reinforced

Unwittingly, this place
affirms the launch of
a life of my own

≈

Ashes

In December the ashes arrived –
in a gold-toned cube with lid ajar
If it is closed, the man said, it will not open again
Now, in July, the ashes rest on a bookshelf
Soon they will go to El Carmelo Cemetery

On a rainy January day, I visited the cemetery –
close to my home, even closer to our home
My cousin was with me

It is not like the rose garden in Westwood
where the ashes of our four parents were scattered
In this rocky windswept terrain, cypress fits better than rose
Here, the gold cube will reside in a concrete chamber
with a wall behind for plaques

In January I bought a place in the memory garden
I had to order a bronze plaque from Pennsylvania
The brochure waited in my desk drawer until this month
when suddenly there was nothing more urgent to do
Soon the plaque will come and the
gold cube will be settled in the cemetery,
its lid firmly closed

That ash on the shelf – what is it of the man?
Even physically a small remnant without
any of the bodily stuff that makes life –
the fluids, the microbes, the multitudes of
mechanical, chemical, electrical processes

It is not the sturdy child who rode his tricycle down the stairs
It is not the tennis player on a summer court

It is not the hiker on a Sierra trail
It is not the warm, brilliant friend, scholar and teacher
It is not the lover of music
It is not the lover

That person lives on. Not in another world but
in a widening circle of lives that he touched,
some in rare, life-changing ways
He taught thousands and some of them taught too

And, for a bit, he lives on
in my memories and my dreams,
in who I am

≈

My Shadows

I live in a bright house,
walk along sparkling shores,
keep house and pay bills,
read books and write poems,
visit with friends,
take classes,
listen to music,
savor my food,
feel great

My shadows live deep in
the hospital in windowless rooms
with pale practitioners who
sit at big computer screens and
never see or speak to patients

My shadows are pictures -
of brain, heart, blood vessels -
and numbers - counts, measures –
of what is in my blood
The pictures were made by
radiation that is not sunlight

It disheartens me that my shadows
are not as healthy as I am, and
I try hard to improve them

But I do not live
in their sealed room
The shadows are there
and I am here - in the
bright bountiful various
sunlit world

≈

Four Haiku. Early pandemic

Haiku: Turning the Calendar Page

March – sunlit field filled
with lupine. April - stream through
dark, steep canyon walls

≈

Haiku. Time of Plague and Flame

Through high window and
smoke, an awful red sun glares
down. It is angry

≈

Haiku. Spider Webs that Went Unseen Before

On mailbox, trash cans,
white with ashes of another
predator's burnt prey

≈

Haiku. A Change of Air

Seen through high window,
a small cloud catches sunlight
My tears surprise me

My Closet in Lockdown

My uniforms are on furlough,
quietly hanging and waiting
for the call back to active duty

Point Lobos uniform -
green jacket with epaulets -
grizzly bear, words in gold thread -
badge in right pocket

Sport center uniform –
black shirt with short sleeves,
black pants with pocket for
iPod loaded with big band jazz

Memoir class uniform –
Nice tee shirt, bright scarf, jeans,
walking shoes – ready for an
after-class walk along Carmel Beach

Concert uniform -
Black pants, light sweater,
shawl or warm scarf,
and a small black purse,
just the right shape
for the program

For lockdown, I dress simply

For walking -
Comfortable tan pants, tee shirt,
athletic shoes, hat, cloth mask, and
one of many old jackets

For home -
Tee-shirt, sweatpants with
pocket for cell phone,
fleece vest or jacket,
comfortable old sandals

No active duty is in sight
but I am patient and
so are my uniforms –
quietly hanging and waiting

≈

Let There Be A Dance

Let there be a time
when we can all cry out
Let there be a dance –
a dance to celebrate survival
a dance to honor the dead

Let the circle of dancers
circle the earth
including those with the least
and those wronged the most

Let the dance go faster and faster
Let it spin off new dances
never danced before

≈

Haiku. January Afternoon on the Dunes

Clouds part. Shadows form.
Sparrows chase theirs. I tail my
tall hooded figure

≈

Haiku. Reading Aloud my Friend's Poems

My friend wrote poems
When I read her words aloud
she still lives in me

≈

Haiku. Spring in Pacific Grove

Spring spreads iceplant-pink
over bluffs, down rocks, onto
brushes and canvas

Instinct

The green-eyed cat,
adopted in maturity for
her amiable disposition,
regularly sharpens her claws,
even though, sometime in her past,
they were removed

≈

Invincible Summer

In the depth of winter, I finally learned that within me there lay an invincible summer. Albert Camus

Winter came on slowly,
over many years
The snow kept falling,
piled ever deeper

A brain was wasting away,
betraying a brilliant witty mind,
undermining a sturdy supple body,
devastating their longtime lover

My life is over, I said
to one I consulted

I was wrong –
despite the grief and the loss,
despite the work and worry

My sleep is deep and
I wake up hungry for the day
The berry is sweet to my tongue,
the air to my lungs
The trail responds to my step and
I respond to a rosy cloud,
a field of flowers, a single poppy,
an old street that descends to the bay
Friends warm my heart
He fills my heart
How can this be?

Camus grew up at the beach and
so did I – over many summers
There must persist, at my core,
those good, slow, easy times of
sun, sand, sea - and summer

≈

My Days at the Beach

I'm with a friend, or two or three
We lie in a line on our towels
Toes toward the water

My towel is anchored by the
big brown radio that I brought
on the bus, down the palisades and
across the highway to the
broad warm creamy sand

The sun, done with its daily
duty to disperse the fog,
warms my oiled skin
dries my wet suit

Thud, whoosh, whisper
Thud, whoosh, whisper
Wave after wave curves, breaks,
slides in foamy

We too have a rhythm

When we are dry and warm
we go down to the water -
cold at first, then not
The waves lift me, gently drop me
Lift and drop, lift and drop until
a big one makes me dive under

We stay until cold and tired
return to the towels, stand and dry,
oil skin, lie prone, turn on music,
get dryer and warmer
turn over
get all dry and too warm
return to water

Repeat until it is late
or the fog comes

Later - a shower,
sleeveless summer dress
to show my even tan

Where has that tan girl gone
the one who surfed and sunned?
Why has she left me here
trudging through gritty gray sand?

Following the Water

Winter storms roll in from the west,
sweeping over Mammoth pass
Snowbanks build and lakes seal up with ice
Between storms the sun's heat deceives and
naïve hikers learn the danger too late

In spring, snowbanks open their taps
Water winds through meadows in tiny streams
and falls to the next level down, into a thawing lake,
and the pattern repeats – inlet to outlet to inlet -
down the ladder of lakes I know so well -
Arrowhead, TJ, Crystal, George, Mary, Twin –
deep blue eyes in glacier-carved granite sockets

And the pattern repeats for other lake ladders
all along the Sierras' sheer East side,
seen from below as narrow green ribbons
                    --
A drop of snowmelt descends the ladder,
rides over Mammoth Falls into Mammoth Creek,
which joins Hot Creek, which makes its way to
the reservoir of the big city's water system, then
through aqueducts and reservoirs to the city,
where I may drink it

And I follow the water's route in
reverse, repeatedly, for most of my life -
driving through desert, then along the base of
the sere range that towers miles above,
reaching a lake, then a higher lake,
following the water to the source

A Letter, Because We Cannot Talk

You were easy to talk to
With you I wasn't shy
Not in the dim college hallway
that first summer
Not on the bright steps
outside that became our
meeting place

You were easy to talk to
for six decades -
and then you weren't

I try monologue when
I can summon the effort
If I talk with another,
at times you listen, at times not
Sometimes you interject a word or two

Music unlocks your voice
When prompted you
remember many songs
Your singing is strong
and strongly felt

Often we sit side by side
to watch a movie – an old one
Often we shed tears together
Yorkshire coal miners lose the
fight for their way of life
Julie in Carousel stands by the
man she unfortunately loves

Often, in those moments,
you reach for my hand
It is then, without words,
that we still talk

Nearing Ninety

Eight years ago I wrote of wonderful women –
over 100, over 90, over 80
I was over 70

Now I'm over 80 and the
one I care for is nearing ninety

He does not arrange flowers
or teach dance or play the piano
He does not walk, rarely talks
but can astound with an apt remark
He paints if someone guides his hand
He plays ball, catching but never throwing
He cries at sad movies and sad songs
And he sings

I don't know what ails his brain
His doctors once thought they knew
and tried to shunt it away
but now say it's not that

What does it matter? He is who he is
Understanding is seen by all who
look into those striking blue eyes

I imagine a phrenology diagram
with shrunken areas for volition and action,
developed ones for empathy and comprehension,
and strands of musicality entwined throughout

Like the centenarian at her piano,

who plays each day each piece she recalls,
he sings his few songs each day
Unlike her, he must be urged

He forgets the words but he knows the tunes

Musings on Beauty

Yesterday, as I walked toward the Asilomar Coast,
I came to a sudden stop when I saw the ocean -
its rich luminescent blues, its continuing wave movement,
the cottony clouds that reflected in the water

Beauty must be an inborn need that we all share -
as with food and water - but we don't die from lack of it

Sex may be a better analogy than food and water
People live long celibate lives, but their sexual needs endure

Today I picnicked on the shore of Monterey Bay,
once more overcome by beauty
The sea was not a rich blue, but a soft gray-blue, quite still
The mountains to the east were a stunning clear purple,
their structure clearly exposed
The hills to the north were beautiful in another way –
in their interaction with soft, horizontal clouds
that hid now one part, now another.

I ate slowly, savoring my luck: I have both a good lunch
and an overflowing bowl of beauty.

≈

After the Rain

After reading Gift by Czeslaw Milosz

Here on the dunes today
every pine, shrub, vine, fern, flower
whispers: I am, I am here

I hear the call of yellow sand verbena,
in its first bloom of the year,
succulent and spreading and bright:
I am here now

Yesterday, yellow-gold poppies,
wide open then, shouted out
Today, I can almost
see their petals open

The sky is pale blue with
scattered thin clouds
On the northern horizon wait
massive stacks of cottony clouds

With each breath I take,
this place colonizes me
With each step I take,
I move closer to
where I belong

A day so happy

On Living Long

My head is a busy buzzing hive -
full of facts, ideas, people, places, events,
songs, films, poems, regrets, joys, hurts,
insights, puzzles

They ooze as bittersweet honey onto
the daily bread of the present

but don't obscure what each today offers:
a fresh ripe fruit that I do my utmost to
savor and devour

≈

Notes

Looking in the Garage. This poem was written in response to one by Naomi Shihab Nye, about searching for a poem, even in the garage.
Being Helen Keller in Whalers Cove. Whalers Cove is in Pt. Lobos State Natural Reserve, on the coast of Central California.
This Fog. This was written when my husband's death was imminent.

Acknowledgments

In 2002, I joined a weekly writing class at the Carmel Foundation that was taught by Illia Thompson. Twenty years later I still attend that class every Wednesday morning. In 2002, I wanted to write poetry, but could not begin. Illia's class was - and is – the perfect place for a beginner. The class heard my wobbly words and responded with only smiles and positive comments – following Illia's guidelines. And so it continues. My gratitude to Illia and the class members over 20 years, and to the Carmel Foundation, is enormous. I am proud that my book will be added to the dozens that have come out of Illia's classes.

For fifteen years I have attended the monthly writing workshops led by Patrice Vecchione at OLLI, the senior education institute at Cal State Monterey Bay. Each month my mind is enriched and stirred by this class and many poems arose there. Thank you, Patrice for your teaching and your inspiration. My deep appreciation also to Michele Crompton, OLLI Program Director, for her elegant management, even in pandemic.

The book and I owe a great debt to the keen readers of early drafts, especially Laszlo Horvath, Carmen Scholis, and Suzanne Cushman. Charlotte Noyes designed the cover, took my photo, and gave other skilled help. Emmanuel Marquez unfailingly resolved software challenges.

My parents and my grandmother, Manya Sharry, made a home full of books and readers. My husband, Stan Summers, brought poetry into my life.